PREVAILING PRAYERS
THAT BREAKS BARRIERS

"God is within her she will not fail! God will help her at the break of day."
Psalms 46:5 (NIV)

QUINCY L. REID

PREVAILING PRAYERS: That Breaks Barriers
Quincy L. Reid

Published 2021 by QL Reid & Co.

All rights reserved. No portion of this book may be reproduced, photocopied, stored, or transmitted in any form-except by prior approval of the publisher.

Unless otherwise noted, all Scripture quotations are taken from the **NEW INTERNATIONAL Version** of the Bible.

U.S. Copyright © 2021 No. 1-10223237531

Printed in the United States of America

ISBN-13: 978-0578870236

Day 1

Forget the former things; do not dwell on the past. See, I am doing a new thing! Now it springs up; do you not perceive it? I am making a way in the wilderness and streams in the wastelands.

Isaiah 43:18-19 (NIV)

Prayer

Abba, I thank you that this is a new day, and you have new things on the horizon for me. My yesterday is a distant memory. My past no longer has a hold on me. I see and feel you are doing new things in, around, and through me. I sense they are bursting and springing forth out of me now.

I thank you that it does not make any difference where I may find myself or be situated throughout my everyday life. You've effectively cleared a path for. I am confident that you will keep on making ways when it may seem there isn't any. I thank you for the new thing in the name of Jesus.

Moment of Reflection

What is the new thing that is springing forth from within you?

_____
_____
_____
_____
_____
_____
_____
_____
_____
_____
_____

Day 2

For I know the plans I have for you, declares the Lord, plans to prosper you and not to harm you, plans to give you hope and a future.

Jeremiah 29:11 (NIV)

Prayer

Abba, I thank you for the plans and purposes you have for my life. They are unique even in this imperfect world. You are my hope and my expectation. The thoughts you have towards me are precious and valuable.

I thank you; my mind is breaking through all the contemplations in opposition to what you have spoken concerning me. I thank you because I'm now embracing my expected end, and I'm currently coming into my new reality in the name of Jesus.

Moment of Reflection

Abba is speaking plans regarding your future. What do you hear?

_____
_____
_____
_____
_____
_____
_____
_____
_____
_____

Day 3

Praise be unto the Lord my Rock, who trains my hands for war, my fingers for battle.

Psalms 144:1 (NIV)

Prayer

Abba, I praise and bless your name today. Thank you for preparing my hands to clap, which delivers a sound of triumph in my breakthrough. I thank you for utilizing my voice to deliver a shout of praise.

I thank you for making my feet that have given me the ability to crush my enemies' head through every trial and tribulation.

Thank you for being my rock and my teacher. I'm breaking through in the name of Jesus.

Moment of Reflection

Is it true that you are prepared for your breakthrough from the fight you were preparing for?

_____
_____
_____
_____
_____
_____
_____
_____
_____
_____
_____
_____

Day 4

So, David went to Baal Perazim, and there he defeated them. He said, "As waters break out, the Lord has broken out against my enemies before me."

2 Samuel 5:20 (NIV)

Prayer

Abba, I thank you for being my present help in any place I may go, thank you for continually being with me.

It is You who reinforce me and empowers me to annihilate, subdue anything or anyone who would oppose me.

I thank you for breaking me through the snares and entanglement of the adversary in the name of Jesus.

Moment of Reflection

Do you feel empowered since you've crushed your adversaries?

_____
_____
_____
_____
_____
_____
_____
_____
_____
_____
_____

Day 5

Ask, and it will be given to you; seek, and you will find; knock, and the door will be opened to you. For everyone who asks receives; the one who seeks finds; and to the one who knocks, the door will be opened.

Matthew 7:7-8 (NIV)

Prayer

Abba, I thank you for your guidance and direction. You've told me to ask, seek and knock. Be persistent in my actions towards receiving the manifestation of my breakthrough.

I thank you that when I ask, breakthrough is given when I seek breakthrough is found and when I knock the door of breakthrough burst wide open to me.

Thank you for causing me to breakthrough in my asking, seeking, and knocking in the name of Jesus.

Moment of Reflection

Since you've asked, seek, and knocked what has broken open to you?

_____
_____
_____
_____
_____
_____
_____
_____
_____
_____
_____
_____

Day 6

The One who breaks open the way will go up before them; they will break through the gate and go out. Their King will pass through before them, the Lord at their head.

Micah 2:13 (NIV)

Prayer

Abba, you are the one who goes before me, breaking the entrance of bronze and cutting through iron bars and steel chains. You clear paths and give protection along the way. You are my battle-ax and my weapon of war. I praise you, incredible God. I rest assure in your promises which stand true now and rings through eternity. Indeed, undoubtedly you are the God of the breakthrough, in the name of Jesus.

Moment of Reflection

At this time, what are those things Abba eliminated from your path? Have you given him praise for doing so?

_____
_____
_____
_____
_____
_____
_____
_____
_____
_____

Day 7

Arise, shine, for your light has come, and the glory of the LORD rises upon you. See, darkness covers the earth, and thick darkness is over the peoples, but the LORD rises upon you, and his glory appears over you.

Isaiah 60:1-2 (NIV)

Prayer

Abba, I will do as you have instructed me, I arise today, I shine today because your glory is upon me. You are the light in this dark, sinful and cold world.

I am your lighthouse that breaks froth and shines radiantly, breaking through the haziness and the fog of life.

Your glory of breakthrough has embellished me and enabled me.

Thank you for your light in the name of Jesus.

Moment of Reflection

Now that the fog has lifted,
what is Abba shinning on for you?

_____
_____
_____
_____
_____
_____
_____
_____
_____
_____
_____

Day 8

Take the helmet of salvation and the sword of the Spirit, which is the word of God.

Ephesians 6:17 (NIV)

Prayer

Abba, Today I put the helmet of salvation on, as it is a fundamental part of my armor that aides me in breaking through.

I utilize the sword of the Spirit, your word, I speak forth because it is alive, sharp, and infiltrates through all hindrance

that would obstruct my breakthrough in the name of Jesus.

Moment of Reflection

What have you sliced through since putting on the helmet and using the sword, the word?

_____
_____
_____
_____
_____
_____
_____
_____
_____
_____

Day 9

They will fight against you but will not overcome you, for I am with you and will rescue you, declares the Lord.

Jeremiah 1:19 (NIV)

Prayer

Abba...You have pronounced my breakthrough from the beginning of time. I, without delay, come in an agreement with your declared word.

Yes, even though the cares of life try to advance toward me, I will not be consumed by it. Thank you for accompanying me. You alone will break me through as you are strong and mighty.

Thank you for being close by my side, and nothing catches you by surprise because you are mindful of the ins and out of my life in the name of Jesus.

Moment of Reflection

What was that thing(s) that attempted to conquer you but could not?

_____
_____
_____
_____
_____
_____
_____
_____
_____
_____
_____

Day 10

"If you hold to my teaching, you are really my disciples. Then you will know the truth, and the truth shall set you free."

John 8:31-32 (NIV)

Prayer

Abba, I am a follower of your word, and you are a man that cannot lie because it goes against your very nature.

Your truth is you, your everlasting word that echoes from the foundation of the earth you created.

I give praise, now that I know your truth, it alerted me, I am a champion, an overcomer, and I hold the title breakthrough in the name of Jesus.

Moment of Reflection

What are some truths you now have in your possession?

_____
_____
_____
_____
_____
_____
_____
_____
_____

Day 11

No weapons forged against you will prevail, and you will refute every tongue that accuses you. This is the heritage of the servants of the Lord, and this vindication from me declares the Lord.

Isaiah 54:17 (NIV)

Prayer

Abba, I know the enemy's desire is to take me out. However, what the enemy construct has planned will not avail itself.

I reject each lie that was sent to bring discouragement and block my coming out and breaking into.

I thank you! Nothing will cease me from apprehending what belongs to me; breakthrough is my portion in the name of Jesus.

Moment of Reflection

Are you able to recall those weapons that were aimed at you, and if so, what were they?

_____
_____
_____
_____
_____
_____
_____
_____
_____
_____
_____

Day 12

I will make you a wall to this people, a fortified wall of bronze; they will fight against you but will not overcome you, for I am with you to rescue and save you declares the Lord.

Jeremiah 15: 20-21 (NIV)

Prayer

I am one who is made of great strength, who stands tall, planted, rooted, and not easily moved.

Even though the confrontation will come, you, oh Lord, are my great deliver, my liberator and knight in shining armor.

Thank you for carefully and skillfully creating me to bring an eruption to the things that would be an impediment to my coming out in the name of Jesus.

Moment of Reflection

What are some things that made you stagnated and prevented you from erupting before this point of your life?

_____
_____
_____
_____
_____
_____
_____
_____
_____
_____

Day 13

Blessed are you, Israel! Who is like you, a people saved by the Lord? He is your shield and helper and glorious sword. Your enemies will cower before you, and you will tread on their heights.

Deuteronomy 33:29 (NIV)

Prayer

Abba, you have truly blessed me! You have protected me. You are the mighty defender that avenges my enemies.

When I call upon your name, your ears are attentive to my voice and come to see about me. Oh, how blessed am I?

You are the glorious sword that reigns, brings breakthrough, justice, and peace to the places it is needed in the name of Jesus.

Moment of Reflection

What was the date(s) or day(s) you remembered seeing your opponent brought to its knees before your very eye?

_____
_____
_____
_____
_____
_____
_____
_____
_____
_____

Day 14

You have delivered me from all my troubles, and my eyes have looked in triumph on my foes.

Psalms 54:7 (NIV)

Prayer

Abba, the Faithful One, who shows His love and kindness towards me.

Just as you rescued David from the lion's paw and the paw of the bear, you will rescue me from all my woes.

My eyes will gaze upon the victory in aww.

Thank you for breaking me loose from all that would try to hold me down in the name of Jesus.

Moment of Reflection

Have you taken a moment to intake all your victories?
If not, take a moment a do so; what are they? How many?

_____
_____
_____
_____
_____
_____
_____
_____
_____
_____

Day 15

From the west, people will fear the Lord's name, and from the rising of the sun, they will revere his glory. For he will come like a pent-up flood that the breath of the LORD drives along.

Isaiah 59:19 (NIV)

Prayer

Abba, I thank you that you are my breath of life, and your glory shines forever.

You pronounced when the enemy comes against me, you will be my high tower, strong, wall of steel.

I thank you for protecting me and being my sure foundation. I do not have anything to fear in the name of Jesus.

Moment of Reflection

What were some of your fears before Abba came on the scene to see about you?

_____
_____
_____
_____
_____
_____
_____
_____
_____
_____
_____
_____

Day 16

Now the Lord is Spirit, and where the Spirit of the Lord is, there is freedom.

2 Corinthians 3:17 (NIV)

Prayer

Abba, I thank you for where your presence abides the breaker's anointing dwells. You, oh Lord, are the way, the truth, and life.

Thank you for being behind me, beside me, and going before me. It is you who is the detonator and explosive, all in one, that shatters the imprisonment of where my breakthrough was held hostage by the enemy.

Thank you, here I am, Lord running to retrieve my blessing in the name of Jesus.

Moment of Reflection

What attempted to detain you from retrieving your blessings? Perhaps it was your own thoughts, or maybe the opinion of others? Whatever it was or possibly is, write it down.

_____
_____
_____
_____
_____
_____
_____
_____
_____
_____

Day 17

And the God of all grace, who called you to his eternal glory in Christ, after you have suffered a little while, will himself restore you and make you strong, firm and steadfast. To him be the power forever. Amen

1 Peter 5:10-11 (NIV)

Prayer

Abba, I hear your call. You are such a gracious and loving God. Here, while living in this earthly realm, I will go through things that may shake my very core.

Nevertheless, there is no doubt in my mind that I will not come out revived and more grounded than previously. The sun that is of our solar system and the SON of God will arise and break forward as a radiant shine in my life. I am thankful to be enveloped in your eternal glory forever.

This is my confidence in you, in the name of Jesus.

Moment of Reflection

Would you say you will endure the weight of life a little longer when it shows up as disappointments, delays, confusion, and frustration, knowing that Glory is on the other side of this?

_____
_____
_____
_____
_____
_____
_____
_____
_____
_____
_____
_____

Day 18

When you passed through the waters, I will be with you; and when you pass through the rivers, they will not sweep over you. When you walk through the fire, you will not be burned; the flames will not set you ablaze.

Isaiah 43:2 (NIV)

Prayer

Abba, your omnipresence brings me harmony and security.

I have dressed myself in the garment of your word, knowing when I pass through the high tide of life, it will not surpass me.

You are in the midst. When the fierce fire of my affairs tries to engulf me, you are my barrier. I am protected and shield by you.

I give you praise; I thank you for continually being close to me and upholding me in the name of Jesus.

Moment of Reflection

What is, or even what were those currents and fiery flames that attempted to devour you but proved unsuccessful?

_____
_____
_____
_____
_____
_____
_____
_____
_____
_____
_____

Day 19

Suddenly an angel of the Lord appeared, and a light shone in the cell. He struck Peter on the side and woke him up. "Quick, get up!" he said, and the chains fell off Peter's wrists.

Acts 12: 7 (NIV)

Prayer

Abba, you are the originator of breaking, losing, and liberating the captives. With the blink of an eye, you orchestrate my freedom. You are my salvation, my saving savior, and the son who sets me free from the shackles that desire to keep me a prisoner.

I give your glory, wonderful Jesus, for releasing me. I thank you for the angelic host company that hearkens unto your commands and excels in strength. Thank you for dispatching them to minister to me and do the bidding on your behalf in the name of Jesus.

Moment of Reflection

What are 3 distinct situations you found yourself in and thought to yourself it would take a long time to break free from?

_____
_____
_____
_____
_____
_____
_____
_____
_____
_____

Day 20

He will call on me, and I will answer him; I will be with him in trouble,

I will deliver him and honor him.

Psalms 91:15 (NIV)

Prayer

Abba, the incredible and mighty defender, has never lost a fight.

I thank you for beckoning to me in my season of distress and knowing my voice as it shouts out to you for help.

I thank you for freeing me once again from the muck and mire soil of life, as you promise you would in the name of Jesus.

Moment of Reflection

What was your latest S.O.S that you communicated to Abba, and he came to your assistance?

_____
_____
_____
_____
_____
_____
_____
_____
_____
_____

Day 21

But the Lord is with me like a mighty warrior; so, my persecutors will stumble and not prevail.

They will fail and be thoroughly disgraced;

Jeremiah 20:11 (NIV)

Prayer

Abba, you are my champion, the great and powerful Lion of Judah, who roars with triumph and authority.

The adversaries who desire my life, you bring them to their knees in defeat.

I thank you for empowering me to win in the faces of my opponents, in the name of Jesus.

Moment of Reflection

What are the emotions you experience when the Lion of Judah comes to the combat zone and fights for you?

_____
_____
_____
_____
_____
_____
_____
_____
_____
_____
_____
_____

Day 22

When the trumpets sounded, the army shouted, and at the sound of the trumpet, when the men gave a loud shout, the wall collapsed; so everyone charged straight in, and they took the city.

Joshua 6:20 (NIV)

Prayer

Abba, you are such a strategic and precise God.

The sound of your voice, which is instrumental, and the insightful counsel you render, caused the surrounding components to possess my breaking forward to collapse and crumble in the name of Jesus.

I thank you for being the trumpet that sounds the alarm as I triumph in the name of Jesus.

Moment of Reflection

Have you missed pertinent information that Abba was giving because you were consumed with what you saw before your eyes?

_____
_____
_____
_____
_____
_____
_____
_____
_____
_____

Day 23

And we know that in all things God works for the good of those who love him, who has been called according to his purpose.

Romans 8:28 (NIV)

Prayer

Abba, you are the Great I Am, that I am who empowers me to leap over the blazing circumstance that would impede my victory.

Although it was intended to bring a hindrance to my deliverance, you worked it out in my favor.

I thank you for your strong hand that brought me out yet again of what should have eliminated me in the name of Jesus.

Moment of Reflection

What was the consuming structure Abba came running into to save you?

_____
_____
_____
_____
_____
_____
_____
_____
_____
_____

Day 24

Blessed is the one who perseveres under trial because, having stood the test, that person will receive the crown of life that the Lord has promised to those who love him.

James 1:12 (NIV)

Prayer

Abba, you said I am blessed because you said it, it is so! Even when things seem to be wreaking havoc and, in an uproar, you said I am blessed.

When my physical body grew weary, and I wanted to quit again, you reminded me I am blessed. I stood and did not cave in. Due to this position and your promise concerning me, I am on the other side.

I thank you for equipping me with the spirit of tenacity that you deliberately placed in me and caused me to thrust forward and over in the name of Jesus.

Moment of Reflection

Did you ever for one moment doubted you were going to be victorious?

_____
_____
_____
_____
_____
_____
_____
_____
_____

Day 25

The Lord your God is with you, the Mighty Warrior who saves. He will take great delight in you; in his love he will no longer rebuke you, but will rejoice over you with signing.

Zephaniah 3:17 (NIV)

Prayer

Abba, I give you praise for the powerful champion you are, the one who saves. Thank you for being my Redeemer, who takes pleasure in and my victories.

Your love for me is genuine and authentic that echoes from earth to eternity in the name of Jesus.

I give glory.

Moment of Reflection

Is there any way you've to hinder Abba from pouring out his blessing upon you that he so richly desires to give you?
If so, list them.

_____
_____
_____
_____
_____
_____
_____
_____
_____
_____
_____

Day 26

But those who hope in the Lord will renew their strength.

They will soar on wings like eagles; they will run and not grow weary,

they will walk and not faint.

Isaiah 40:31 (NIV)

Prayer

Abba, you are the one who ascends and launches. My expectations are in you and you alone, while in my fatigued state, you ceaselessly reestablish my strength.

I thank you for the surge of your power that is distributed throughout my body.

I will not be depleted or faint when I move along rocky trails of life in the name of Jesus.

Moment of Reflection

Have you taken off on the wings of Jesus?
If you have, what is your evidence?
If not, for what reasons haven't you?

_____
_____
_____
_____
_____
_____
_____
_____
_____
_____

Day 27

The name of the Lord is a fortified tower; the righteous run to it and are safe.

Proverbs 18:10 (NIV)

Prayer

Abba, you are my strength like no other. Your name protects me from the components and cruelty of life.

I thank you that I can run to you, and you welcome me wholeheartedly,

and all fear and worries are a distant memory in the name of Jesus.

Moment of Reflection

How is the name of the Lord a strong tower, a safe haven for you?

_____
_____
_____
_____
_____
_____
_____
_____
_____
_____

Day 28

Nehemiah said, "Go and enjoy choice food and sweet drinks, and send some to those who have nothing prepared. This day is holy to our Lord. Do not grieve, for the joy of the Lord is your strength."

Nehemiah 8:10 (NIV)

Prayer

Abba, the transcendent God who turns my mourning into gladness.

At the mention of your very name, it ushers in joy and laughter, which are medicine to my soul during strenuous times.

I thank you for being my might and empowering me to be joyful when it appears as though I should be downtrodden in the name of Jesus.

My fortified pillar is who you are.

Moment of Reflection

Have you encountered this joy?
Wait, really experienced it?
If so, what were the surrounding events of that occasion?

_____
_____
_____
_____
_____
_____
_____
_____
_____
_____

Day 29

The voice of the Lord breaks the cedars; the Lord breaks in pieces the cedars of Lebanon.

Psalms 29:5 (NIV)

Prayer

Abba, you are the boundless God who surpasses our human understanding and computation. Your voice obliterates, shatters, and demolishes the very thing that you made.

My God, who is like you, Lord, undeniably no one!

I thank you for your amplified voice that speaks and battles for me in the name of Jesus.

Moment of Reflection

What was an event that the Lord crushed the true spirit of your adversary?

_____
_____
_____
_____
_____
_____
_____
_____
_____
_____

Day 30

The Lord will deliver them to you, and you must do to them all that I have commanded you. Be strong and courageous.

Do not be afraid or terrified because of them,

for the Lord your God goes with you; he will never leave you nor forsake you.

Deuteronomy 31:5-6 (NIV)

Prayer

Abba, I thank you for making my foes bow. I thank you for always being by my side.

I can laugh in their faces, despite the fact they desired to sift me.

However, they cannot touch me in the name of Jesus.

I am bold, fearless, and well protected by you.

Thank you for calling me to the procession of victory..

Moment of Reflection

How do you know that God is present in your life?

_____
_____
_____
_____
_____
_____
_____
_____
_____
_____

Day 31

"I have told you these things, so that in me you may have peace.

In this world you will have trouble.

But take heart! I have overcome the world."

John 16:33 (NIV)

Prayer

Abba, the immutable God who has always been and will always be. I thank you for each fight at any point I could encounter. You have effectively won it for me by completion work on the cross in the name of Jesus.

You defeated this world with your blood and sacrifice at Calvary. I can take comfort and be in peace knowing I have already won and every one of my adversaries are crushed; as a result, you.

I give you praise, I give you glory, for you are the true and living God who redeems. Mighty is your name throughout eternity.

Moment of Reflection

Since you have completed this 31-day venture, how do you feel? Has anything changed? If so, what has?

_____
_____
_____
_____
_____
_____
_____
_____
_____
_____
_____
_____

Conclusion

My prayer and desire that this book from day 1 to day 31 have empowered, inspired, and equipped you in a more excellent way with the word of God as your weapon of warfare.

Beloved, you are victorious and a champion in Christ, in the name of Jesus.

Blessings to you,
Quincy

If you'd like to follow me on my social media page, you can reach out to:

FB @ QLReid

Or email me at:

QLReid44@gmail.com